BUSHIDO
The Virtues of Rei and Makoto

Essays and Poems

Also by Arthur Stewart

Rough Ascension and Other Poems of Science

BUSHIDO
The Virtues of Rei and Makoto

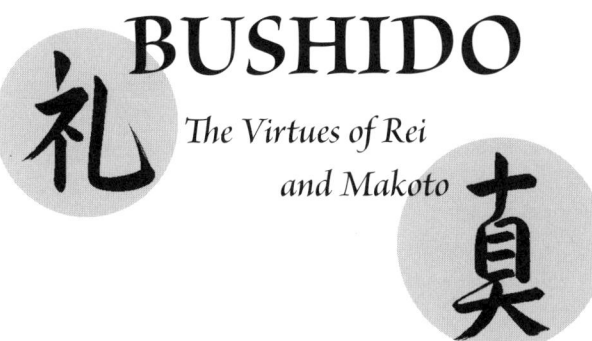

Essays and Poems by

Arthur J. Stewart

Celtic Cat Publishing
KNOXVILLE, TENNESSEE

© 2005 Arthur J. Stewart

All rights reserved. No part of this publication may be reproduced, stored in a retrieval system, or transmitted in any form or by any means—electronic, mechanical, photocopy, recording, or other—except for brief quotations in written reviews, without the prior written permission of the publisher.

Celtic Cat Publishing
PO Box 23694
Knoxville, Tennessee 37933–1694
www.celticcatpublishing.com

We look forward to hearing from you. Please send comments about this book to the publisher at the address above. For information about special educational discounts and discounts for bulk purchases, please contact Celtic Cat Publishing.

Manufactured in the United States of America

Acknowledgments: "Law of Chemistry" (poem) and "Trickster Rules" (essay) previously appeared, in slightly different form, in *Chemical Intelligencer* and *Big Muddy: A Journal of the Mississippi River Valley*, respectively. The author thanks the editors of these periodicals.

ISBN: 0-9658950-6-8

Library of Congress Control Number: 2005923461

For Robert G. Wetzel

*who took the time to teach me
the art of science and to show me,
by example, how to get things done*

Contents

Preface	xi
The Concept of Bushido	xiii

Rei

How to Take Care of a Stream	3
Ghanaian Story	6
Here to Stay	11
Bushido	14
How to Do It	25
Japanese Beetles	27
Attention to Detail	28
Becoming Bushido	30
Making a Difference	33
Threading the Needle	35
Rat Dissection	37
Law of Chemistry	39
A New Way to Generate Respect	41
Bewept with Disrespect	43
It Lives	44
Dark Water	48

 Makoto

Trickster Rules	53
Fat as the Moon	58
An Honest Mistake	60
The Truth	62
Belly of the Beast	64
Bias	66
Brier Creek	67
Einstein Was Right Again	68
Lost Water	69
Finale on the Finger	70
You Know You Never Know	72
News by Phone	73
When Electricity Goes Off at Night	74
Recalibration Might be Needed	75
Perspective on the Destruction of Mossy Grove	77
Two Sides of the Coin	79
About the Author	80

Preface

A single theme focuses the essays and poems within this book—respect and care for life in this world of ours. This theme is captured in spirit by the concept of Bushido, the samurai way of life: Bu (martial arts), shi (warrior), and do (the way).

The essays and poems in *Bushido* developed as natural outgrowths of my scientific background. The style, diction and language are similar to those found in my first book, *Rough Ascension and Other Poems of Science*. However, *Bushido* includes several longer poems that allow me to better capture the dips, swoops, loops and swirls that make up the connections of our nubby little individual lives. Archie Ammons, a writer whose poems I greatly admire, was a master at capturing these dynamic nonlinearities:

> . . . the mirrorments, astonishments of mind,
> what are they to the natural phenomena, the gross destructions
> that give life, we cooling here and growing on a far outswing
>
> of the galaxy, the soaring, roaring sun in its thin-cool
> texture allowing us, the moon vacant though visitable, Mars
> not large enough to hold an air, Venus too hot, so much
>
> extravagance of waste, how can the bluegreen earth look
> purposeful, turn a noticeable margin to meaning: what are
> mirrorments, then, so shatterable, liable to melt, too
>
> much light, the greasy graying of too much time: man waited
> 75,000 years in a single cave (cold, hunger, inexplicable
> visitation of disease) only to rise to the bright, complex
> knowledge of his destruction![1]

To set the scene, I provide some background information on the concept of Bushido.

---

1. From *Sphere: The Form of a Motion*, pp. 30–31.

The Concept of Bushido

Samurai warriors emerged as the elite ruling class in Japan during the 1400s and 1500s, and these men lived by moral principles today collectively referred to as Bushido. The concept of Bushido grew from the fusion of Buddhism and Shintoism and, based on retrospective analyses, rests on seven virtues:

Gi	the right decision
Yu	bravery and courage
Jin	benevolence
Rei	respect
Makoto	truth and sincerity
Meiyo	honor
Chugo	loyalty and devotion

While the essence of a samurai's life lay in acquiring skills in the art of war and practicing Bushido, in times of peace he also cultivated more genteel pursuits. The art of Cha no Yu, or the tea ceremony, became perhaps the most popular mode of artistic expression with the samurai class as a whole, but poetry, calligraphy and other literary arts attracted samurai devotees as well. Many samurai became accomplished poets. Minamoto Sanetomo (1192–1219), the third Kamakura shogun, published an anthology of his poems, the *Kinkaishu*, and Taira Tadanori (1144–1184), the younger son of Taira Kiyomori, achieved fame as a poet. Even during the constant fighting of the Sengoku Jidai, some samurai developed artistic talents to match their martial accomplishments. Date Masamune (1567–1636), the overlord (daimyo) of Sendai in northern Honshu, was so moved by the beauty of Mt. Fuji that he wrote:

Each time I see Fuji,
It appears changed
And I feel I view it
Ever for the first time.

During the 1600s, warring ceased in Japan and there was a time of unification. By the late 1700s, Japan had started moving towards a more modernized and western way of life, further reducing the need for samurai. The samurai and their way of life were abolished officially in the early 1870s.

The reality of Bushido, of course, is far more intricate than suggested by this thin outline. Bushido has come to mean different things to different people. When the samurai were at their strongest, Bushido was not codified; it consisted, at best, of a few maxims handed down from mouth to mouth or from the pen of some well-known warrior or savant. Bushido grew organically, over decades and centuries. The Bu-shi (Fighting Knights) emerged slowly as a privileged class, and at first were likely a rough breed who made fighting their vocation. Over a long period of near-constant warfare, this class survived, establishing families and the ranks of the samurai. Coming to profess honor and privilege, and corresponding responsibilities, they began to feel the need for a common standard of behavior, today expressed in the word, Bushido. The codification of its principles actually occurred well after the samurai's role had diminished, during the 17th and 18th centuries.

According to Inazo Nitobe (1863–1933), Bushido was the maker and product of Old Japan and a guiding principle and formative force of the transition to the new era:

> Have you seen in your tour of Japan many a young man with unkempt hair, dressed in shabbiest garb, carrying in his hand a large cane or a book, stalking about the streets with an air of utter indifference to mundane things? He is the shosei (student), to whom the earth is too small and the heavens are not high enough. He has his own theories of the universe and of life. He dwells in castles of air and feeds on ethereal words of wisdom. In his eyes beams the fire of ambition; his mind is athirst for knowledge. Penury is only a stimulus to drive him onward; worldly goods are in his sight shackles to his character. He is the repository of loyalty and patriotism. He is the self-imposed guardian of national honour. With all his virtues and his faults, he is the last fragment of Bushido.

The concept of Bushido was brought to the western world primarily through Nitobe's book *Bushido: The Soul of Japan*, first published in 1899. This book became not only an international bestseller, but served as the cornerstone for the construction of an edifice of ultra-nationalism that led Japan down the path to a war she did not win. Nitobe had an American wife, became a Christian, and studied in the United States for three years, then in Germany for three more years before returning to Japan to write *Bushido*.

The essays and poems in this book highlight two of the seven Bushido virtues—Rei (respect), and Makoto (truth and sincerity). The term Rei translates unambiguously to respect, or to bow as a show of respect. However, the translation of Makoto is more complex. Makoto derived originally from the terms "ma" (meaning true) and "koto," meaning words or things. But like Bushido, Makoto has taken on a wider range of meaning: in addition to truth, honesty and sincerity, the term Makoto has developed deep connotations of a personal, unwavering commitment, without desire for fame or acknowledgment—a sense of truth as the natural state of being.

The elements of Rei and Makoto should, I believe, have a special influence in society today. They are powerful tools which, if applied conscientiously by individuals, would go a long way towards overcoming global divisiveness. Consistent application of these attitudes in daily life also would help address some of our more pressing environmental and intercultural problems.

References

Ammons, A. R. 1974. *Sphere: The Form of a Motion.* W. W. Norton & Company, New York, NY.

Nitobe, I. 2001. *Bushido: The Soul of Japan.* 2nd ed., digitalized January 17, 2001, by Teresa Corp.

Rei

Respect

How to Take Care of a Stream

I live in Lenoir City, a small town southwest of Knoxville, Tennessee—Appalachia, pure and simple, in the ridge and valley province. But the area is urbanizing rapidly now due to its proximity to several key interstate highways. This rapid growth in population means change, and change, in turn, can set the stage for conflict.

It is a hot, still morning in late July. Clouds already are piling up to the west, suggesting the likelihood of an afternoon thunderstorm. I'm with a fellow stream ecologist, Mike Ryon; we have a group of seven high school students in tow. I'm in calf-high olive-green rubber boots; Mike and the students are in chest waders. We're walking now near the edge of an area that has been leveled recently to make a soccer field, not far from the town's high school. Stripped of its vegetation, the land has been scraped to hard clay. From high in the air, I think, it might look like a very small version of the Great Red Spot on Jupiter: it is that color—red-orange-yellow. Having been leveled, the field lacks natural contour: it is flat; it has no ecological personality. But it is bordered on the north and the east by Town Creek, and Town Creek, this morning, is our destination.

Along the northern edge of the field, near the stream, I show the students how an improperly installed silt curtain fails to prevent silt from running from the field directly into the stream. The black mesh curtain is staked firmly and it looks snug and smug at a distance. But the base of the curtain is not buried, and clearly it had not been buried even when it was installed. Already there are telltale signs of erosion. Here and there, water has cut little gullies into the red clay under the curtain—little places that bleed silt into the stream with even a small rain. Straw bales have been deployed to help prevent the flux of silt to the stream when it rains. These bales also look good at a distance. But they are poorly staked and not properly placed. Most of the bales are non-functional with respect to their intended purpose: they have no chance of intercepting any surface flow at all, even in the event of a hard rain. The students absorb these details; they consider the evidence; they discuss the situation; they express indignation. They do not respect what has been done.

Mike points out various invasive plant species thriving along the stream's bank—privet, Japanese grass, kudzu, Japanese honeysuckle, Johnsongrass. He explains how invasive plants can out-compete native vegetation, reducing biodiversity and lowering the quality of food and habitat available for wildlife. The students look and listen.

A few dozen meters farther, I pause again and point out to the students with a sweeping hand the curve of a large sycamore tree. It leans gracefully over the stream, roots gripping a steep undercut bank. Mike explains how trees and bushes can stabilize stream banks with their roots; I talk about how the canopies of the trees shade the stream, keeping the water cooler. We work our way next through a scruffy zone of ironweed, oxeye daisies and Queen Anne's lace, then plunge to shade under trees, passing through a smattering of jewelweed, poison ivy and monkey flower. Then, at last, in deep shade, we come to water.

There, Mike points out the main features of stream structure—pools, runs and riffles, all snuggled into the stream channel. These structures are held in place by the interaction of bedrock, the mass of moving water and gravity. We squat in the stream to capture a few snails, find a crawdad, measure the temperature of the water and collect a water sample for laboratory analysis; we turn over a few rocks to see what's there. Then Mike gets the battery-powered backpack electrofisher fired up. He wades into the pool with the shocker and goes at it, nudging the long-handled probes behind and under fallen limbs, around rocks, boulders and cobbles, nosing them into secret places where stream fish like to hide. He works slowly upstream, through the pool, through a riffle, through the next pool. The students wade in single file behind him. Three make themselves busy netting stunned fish. They put the fish they net into a plastic five-gallon bucket, half-full of water.

Seventy meters or so later, the stream bends hard to the right. We stop there, at the base of a large pool, in the shade of a sycamore. Fish and water in the bucket are poured into a dip net. The water runs through the net, revealing a wiggling, thrashing collection of fish. Mike sorts them quickly by species, pointing out differences in the position of their mouths, differences in coloration, differences in body plans. Each fish, an individual: hogsuckers, white suckers, stoneroller minnows, striped shiners, bluegill sunfish, blacknose dace, snubnose darters, creek chubs and lots and lots of banded sculpins. Each fish is identified before being released back into the stream. A student tallies the number of fish of each type as they are released. As he works through the fish, Mike explains new terms he uses in describing the catch: "pollution tolerant," "benthic," "fusiform" and "omnivorous." He explains how the various types of fish found here do things differently, and how, although they are individuals, they work together as a community.

Something behind us moves and almost as one we turn to look back.

There, two pools downstream, at the bend where we started, a great blue heron has landed. It folds its wings carefully, then stands motionless, staring at us warily from stream's edge. The students stop what they are doing. All seven stand motionless, staring back. After a moment they begin talking again, but more quietly now. Today we've shown them stream Bushido: form and function; attention to detail; individuals, communities; respect the water, honor the land. We've done what we can with this little group of Appalachian high school students. Five years from now, or ten years perhaps, after they've settled down and become productive individual members of society, they may remember how to take care of a stream.

Ghanaian Story

Kwami

Growling bear of a black man, Kwami swings
his massive head left and right, bright eyes
buried in a coarse face, gaze searing the underbrush: he has
the perverse will of a hungry man in a desperate place.
Huge buttressed trees he hacks and girdles to bring down
a little burst of light-patch. Lianas, pulled, slashed
by machete, thick as an arm are oozing: they get dragged and stacked.
They smolder; a crackle of wet smoke crawls from the tangle.

Things grow
practically as fast as he can cut. I stand sweating just watching him
ripping a gardening place by the home. His wife is growing
a confabulation of yams: their soft green tendrils
creep up bamboo poles, minor hope
blasted dark each afternoon. He wants to grow
maize, okra and tomatoes but the huge trees
near the garden's edge are too dominant.

Today clouds take all morning
pushing up, lusty white
mushrooms of energy: later the drops
come huge and fall slow. They hang
suspended as they fall, each
drop is its own thing, coming
suddenly together in a rushing roar: binding
to one another, joining
the sounds of drops, mingling—
they speak in many little voices. In the rain for a moment
Kwami just stands there, breathing, listening.

After the rain: the murmur of children,
the smoke of lianas lingering. And always

the yams, pallid masses dug from the thin red dirt in season,
steamed or boiled or baked, or stewed or souped. He, Kwami,
still standing, but now

in the doorway of the dark hut,
rattled loose to thunder, looking out
past roof-thatch, past the papaya tree, into the forest,
into the afternoon made dark luminescent
by rain receding.

The fish call with no voice

After the rain I walk to the edge of a pond a short way
into the forest: the fish call
somehow with no voice. I see them slipping
pale as yams, back and forth

in the water like smoke. The pond
is dark and motionless: it is
holding its breath; it seems pinned
to the forest floor by the lilies, thick at the edge.

A bird calls, then quiet. My heart lurches like a blind thing,
though glancing back towards Kwami's hut I can see
rooftop: rare rain-free
afternoon sun glinting

from the clearing. The only sound
this instant, somewhere,
trickling water.
Then

more sound, motion. Four children chattering,
from Kwami's house; naked but for tattered shorts

come towards the pond to watch: their voices
like birdcalls, a vine winding nowhere. In the pond

the fish move
just under the water; they seem to be counting
the slow strokes of their fins;
they are coming

like children
now through the stems of the lilies, towards me, opening
and closing their mouths,
staring —

I do not know how they know
but they move
closer, their mouths, the light
and shadows working together

in the luminescent world of green and black, the fish
silver, in silence. They come to me and I, mindless
god of do-good then
plunge the arm and grab one by the gill-cover and jerk

the heavy body to the light, up
flopping hard bankside, silver on shadow,
sides heaving, red gills gripping
solidly at empty air, the mouth

opening and closing now my heart
lunging in time to the bird-call
chattering of children
arriving, excited.

Pride spills through me like an uprush of rain backwards: food,
beyond the pale of yam, cheap rice,
onions and lean black beans, the wet fish
still thrashing weakly.

Trophy home

Hooking fingers under gill-cover the wetness
bleeds down my hand; I swing the timeless symbol of trophy-catch;
I feel pure, slimed joyful to bird-call perfection.

A thing is wrong and set to right

Kwami lunges from the dark of hut-house reeking of palm wine, eyes
wide blazing, clarion face a storm of disbelief stumbling anger, staring
   at the fish
hanging from my hand: the dead soul
of an ancestor: his father's father, his mother's mother, or older brother,
or brother of brother, maybe; he reeks and rants, the bird-calls
of the motley children gone,

the sun
slamming now hard bars of light,
the words crash the high trees, the clouds
still pushing up away; his woman
bent hoeing yam hills straightens, tightens her cloth, stands silent
yet things
still green in the silver shadows.

I am emptied completely. We talk
for a long time that afternoon, settling until fireflies
work together at dusk, punctuating the calls of the new night
   with small

speckles of hope. It takes two big calabashes of fresh palm wine
    and a full
bottle of Schnapps to right the wrong and the fish

we bury at last, drunk,
staggering to the yam field
together, machetes swinging dangerously digging random holes
    in darkness.

Here to Stay

Up or down, around and around, things
in motion, whirling, the living world

beat up and knocked down but
constantly rising nonetheless:

between rain events today
a blue sky, white clouds, the sun

rolling in and the wet grass
growing so fast it creaks at the joints

like corn in a field at night: Bushido: roll the word
in your mouth, let it melt

like a pat
of butter; swallow it, feel it

slide and swell in the belly and trickle up
the arms, tingle the brain: you might

use a samurai sword to cut
underbrush but I prefer

a machete—put an edge
on that tool and she'll work

with you all day. In Ghana, students bent
their backs and cut

schoolyard grass with machetes, swooping
arcs so the multiple blades from the multiple

strong black arms glistened

like the sun, the headmaster's stern

glare overseeing the work-
force: monkeys chattering

in gnarly trees, everything getting
spruced up for an official visit. But still

Bushido: three syllables, one
after another — not

country specific, not
climate specific, not

this, not that, but still
it works so respect it

for things technological, things
scientific and social, probably

things political though that thought
might be an abomination today, when

warriors under various flags, some sporting
stars or moons stylized to the point of being

something other than what they're supposed to
represent, oh my

    goodness! such a tizzy

but the old sphere
keeps turning, not caring a whit about

what flag is where, except
we're getting warmer, you know:

global warming is here for a long while.

Bushido

For Archie Ammons

1

Ah, take words,
basalt or fault, has or had, anything
shaking the compass-point from north
wobbling to the steady pull of electromagnetic

force generated by the spinning earth
alone or in combination
with composition: the slow slosh of a molten iron core
feeling its way under molten stone and that

feeling its way under stone and rock
heated putty-soft and that
feeling its way to warm rock solid and steady and such
layering goes on right to the top where it

2

radiates now
long-wave to the night, giving off heat sucked up
by day under the slow spin, this face
then that, to the sun, bathed

to perfection periodically by the solar flux
surging
episodically from steady, flurry and storm
from the sky down

into the earth, well-ward, steened or not,
again like the beginning

of Archie Ammons' *Sphere:*
The Form of a Motion but note:

3

he used twelve lines to the set,
four groups of three, one hundred
fifty-five sets to say
cutting to the chase

he's off at last, sailing. Now this
picking up where he left off: passing down
through the discrete to the general, I say yes we can
rise back to the rarified

discrete, the slim and delicate
particulars, the flower parts of the lily, the teasing
separations of chromosomes used to get
to the haploid state — flimsy

4

sure, but even DNA is
more substantial than single molecules
disconnected, Brownian motion, bouncing
in water or air, and these entities are comprised of course

of smaller parts — electrons, protons,
neutrons, and these are formed
in turn of quarks, and so on
to who knows where — radiation again

I guess. I can see now
why he used colons, studly
stoppers, cuff links
to snug things up, tie things off

5

starched sleeves, closed at the right place. Otherwise
things might
go if they weren't tied down—
whirl off

perhaps or sink, that's it
rising or falling, choppy or smooth,
devolving constantly
to vectored choice

in wavelength, the amount of energy
in a pack of light: it might
excite an atom, so the atom takes it in and gives off
light of longer wavelength

6

shifting
the color we see
flowing now from the tiger lily
back to the eyes

black spots
burning the flower's face of orange.
He wrote
on average just five point one lines per day, surely

I could do that, do you think? Maybe
but then I find his lines were longer: in this,
mine are more strip-like, compressed, enjambed
tight to the wall, like his later work. Reminding me:

7

push it back to where it needs to go: circle out
tentacle-like, the sensitive tip
probing the surface, feeling the edge, a crevice,
a small crack

invisible to the eye but still seeable
given the right dose of the right
radiation again: and more
stoppage, wanted or not, the tentacle

lets me try tenticular, not there but
tentaculoid occurs, sure
but the point is
words around it pertain

8

also to the problem at hand: how to express
the trembling little thing that feels
through time or space a change
tentative, tentaculum, tensor, tensive

tension of course, even tenotomy
might help, the cutting or division of a tendon
(subcutaneous thing of attachment)
by a surgeon's slender knife. Or forward

to tentiginous, that being
provocative or excited to lust and on
finally to tenuous, the state
I'm trying to get past. All the way

9

to teratolite, from the name you can tell
a mineral — an impure
clay-like hydrous silicate of aluminum
back towards earth again

and Archie's tendency to avoid
commonalities, things of his own making. It is water
still in any case and thus it contains
the proper intrinsic properties, lacking just

motion imposed
by gravity and light, naught else
holds the bird up poised
this instant on molecules of air.

10

See, if I did this for just 16 days I'd have him beat
on the basis of rate at least, rate being
change in distance or amount per unit time and time's
where I try to shine. Hell

we (in the royal sense) work routinely
now in femtoseconds,
fractional bits of 10 to the minus 15 seconds
and that is short let me tell you

or if you'd like to go long
for a pass, truck out
to the big bang: through the crackle and hiss
of things created

11

some 15 billion years ago and calculating
that in seconds I get four point seven
times ten to the seventeenth, the total
operating range of time

in seconds therefore being
something like ten
raised to the power of 32, enough
to take you

wherever you might want to go
mostly. But that's not fair, either:
powers of ten won't get you
to love

12

and it lets death hang there
instantaneously, forever: tessellate that
if you can or slice
the cone to generate

circles, ovals, hyperbolas, so many things
exist outside of time, its OK
to spatterdock the world, recede
to archipelagos, islands slung down

from the blue above into the blue
below, or rising up, bounded by water, salt
or fresh, supporting trees or grass or if not this
then another form of life.

13

Bringing things
in a way to the first whole circle done.
Yet not done for the system spirals
constantly up or down, direction depending

upon the point of view, frivolous or serious,
tollent, that meaning, to take away
or to negate, and its opposite, that of
adding to: or turdiform

not what you think, I bet, but meaning
robin-shaped from the Linnean,
Turdus migratorius, contrasted to
— what — ? A non-flying thing

14

wet perhaps, boneless and which sleeps
underground: does not produce
blue-shelled eggs, does not
have feathers, lacks

a beak, feet, a shining yellow-ringed eye —
see: failing to set the ends we still set
comparisons, this to that, arbitrary
axes for scaling

impossible things to each other, this
our delight, our love, our perpetual
proclivity for prevarication, we want
to elaborate for understanding.

15

Thus reaching back
to layers, laminations
next to lamp, designed to illuminate
crevices, cracks, pits, pores, hair-line

fractures: the plastering up, the sealing in,
delectable detection of flaw, determined by
comparison, the whole body
of statistics formulated for this

singular purpose, stated objective to reduce
uncertainty in what we think we know
by god to some specified
level of comfort and note this word

16

contains fort: bastion
of protection, safety, accountability, a structure
designed to resist, a wall
for example of a spore or plant cell

enclosing more tentative things
inside, processes or items that need
protection: controlled conditions,
a regulated flux—

desired things in, non-useful things out,
again to the back and forth sway, the dynamic
pendulum of being—not defiance
against entropy, no not that, it's constantly

17

more towards love. I'm wondering here
can I let line length grow precisely to accommodate
complications and combinations, the essential set of elaborations
needed for sustainability: swooping integrals, the expanded reach, the
    attempt to detect

what's out there, beyond the tip of, like Nabakov once said, that
    tentaclinging wet hair?
If it is a body drifting, face down so as to rise and fall delicately with
    each gentle swell
with ripples or waves too small to be called waves rolling sometimes
up over the glistening skin then sliding off, each water molecule
    clinging first to another

water molecule, each being slightly negative on one side, slightly
    positive on the other,
each rolling in constant motion, turning themselves to the body first,
    then back
to water, reluctant, to some degree, to break loose, to let go until
hammered by light: until assimilating the packet

18

of light having energy sufficient to break
the water-to-water attractive bonds, setting one free
to air, at least
closing

circle two, in part. Now off
gradation — look
for the abrupt transition: the popping up
of the fiddlehead in spring, the yellow violet

that by a twisting pod shoots its seeds
pow! tens of centimeters
somewhere to the forest floor: or snake-strike,
head blurring to the frog

19

motionless — that is rate: a circle again. I can't think
outside time I guess
like the cubistic nude in blues and grays trapped
descending the staircase,

instantaneous motionless motion, shape
of life, the color of sound, a weak force
centering the strong
molecular basis for love.

It is not possible to tessellate
points. It is clouding up
outside, the cool front that pushed in
surprising us in mid-summer has

20

completed itself: it drew back, recursed: humid air
hurrying north now, warm from the south and the sun
centers too: no
red eye, no cauldron of morning

blistering the heart—rather, a ghostly globe high
and in this beautiful solar sphere I see reflected
the form of a motion: either from nothing or bastardized
from Bushido, temporarily, Bushido I name you,

living thing I do not know
other than by words given to me by those skimming
earthly things that touch and move on touch,
these two hundred and forty lines, Archie, I write for you.

How to Do It

From the ideal of Bushido,
we have moral obligations
to respect the earth,
to get it as right as possible:

the high and the low
the shimmering and the parts
that grind rock-like against one
another, the pieces that fit from years

of adaptation, and those that don't
now and never will: continuing,
a set of imperatives that can't be
defined in unambiguous terms, at least

not to perfection, a fuzzy set though some rules
we've figured out and use
to societal benefit. Aluminum for example
can be alloyed with lithium, and a bacterial gene

for citrate synthase can be put into
the roots of plants, thus reducing
the bioavailability of aluminum
in soil to plants, a good thing

for papayas that would otherwise
sicken and die. But these advances leave
a blinding hole: a place black
as hell, into which we must dive individually, yet

before so doing it is essential to strip
off pretensions: shed these, one

after another like shucking corn, starting
at the top of the ear, pulling down to reveal

pearly young sweet
cream or yellow, the tender new
parts of the self that are gold
and good and which might

with luck pass on
to feed us, the collective: in honor of all
we have been, we might be, the heights
to which we, individuals of the collective, aspire.

Japanese Beetles

So many leaves of the beautiful
linden trees have come down

this summer
skeletonized by the damned

Japanese beetles
unaware of Bushido

but warriors in their own way
they work assiduously at mating, one

glistening bronze body on another,
thrusting hind legs out stiff

when alarmed: their enemy
my friend, malathion

in water rises in a spray, drips
leaf to leaf but slows them only.

They attend to life; they are intent
on living.

Attention to Detail

I have concerns
about enjambment and the splitting
of words. Should it be, for example, cork-
screwed, or corkscrewed? Details

are so important. And what about the frequent use
of colons, of the punctuation variety?
Studly cuffs, good for terminating
ideas, fractured lines — they behave

like bookends: hold things
together tight but
if overtapped do they lose
effectiveness? Now back — the damned

road here, where I'm driving, now — it goes
up and left around the hill, almost half
a mile. This is where they dribbled
hot stuff, radiologically speaking,

from a tanker truck. Liquid radioactive waste
dribbled setting off
pancake meters, alarms, whoa, sez they, them little
spots got some serious mustard on'em. Later,

men in white coats surveyed the hill:
they checked car tires, too. Gravity
wins again. But like I said
the road

looks now like a dog with mange: black
patches of fresh asphalt pressed smooth

where concrete pieces had to be
chipped out so they could be taken to a special place,

a dump for hot stuff. An accidental
accident; a bad decision, or
inadequate attention to detail.

Becoming Bushido

1

The process should be broken
into little steps: the getting ready
parts are the most important—
they are at least parts
as important as the white
chicken standing beside the red

wheelbarrow, you know the rest.
It is that level of precision that's needed:
each feature of each thing trimmed
to the essence and once that's done

the next step: the one
best done with the eyes closed
and the everlasting thought of purity streaming up
from the gut through the brain and out
the top and down you go. Forget

the physical manifestation
of what we do with the earth, collectively
and as individuals: just sink
into the black hole of the self: this precedes
the production of garbage. From threads
of nothing, something emerges.

2

Thus deeper, past old things known
or which were remembered once
but were then forgotten: some
brief sparkle attracts, I can't take

a week to get there — a line or two only
will have to do and this should let you know

the problem of intensification. The acute
compression of action, the steady
pressure applied to make progress — things
pile up, get hooked
together, threaded or tied, snagged,
bottled, boxed and belted
to other things, no space
between to allow the definition of one
thing or condition from another, too
tight, everything wedged
like on a strip: can't get
even a finger-

nail into a crevice to wedge
into the tiny split, a crack, stress
leading to a fracture, place where
molecules have flat given up
their hold to one another, said
electrostatically speaking,

shit, forget about it. Let
go. That's

where the real fall starts.
Do not plan
to soar like a turkey
vulture peering down as you
circle deeper. It is not
like that: it lacks

the grace of a feather, the nudge

of breeze and remember

it is dark. Probably
I could give an advance report
on conditions: the temperature
for example is such-and-such,
the humility should be exactly
one hundred percent. But
these are insubstantial cover-ups,
sweet fluffs
to distract the mind while the real work
has to be done so it's best
to get going. After some time,
I can't tell you how long, it varies
from one person to the next
you can begin

to live
again,
the right way. One
atom at a time,
you can begin putting
love in a beautiful world.

Making a Difference

It's June and I should take back
now what I said earlier, the words

about falling
into the self and paths in the dark

and all that other crap
about exploring things internal: today

I think mindless
might be a better Bushido way to go: creep

over the crannies, cracks and fractured
bits of rock: hold

nothing back, don't
look too hard for meaning

in the vagaries of life, the larger swoops
might be worth a glance or two,

it depends. This morning a tough
decision: sugar, chocolate or honey

into the coffee black: well, honey won
at last, and I fetched a handful

of walnuts, halves and pieces, to round
things out and out of the blue — *ding*! the new

Gilbert mantel clock, in actuality an old clock
recently renovated and made to run

like new let loose its half-hour chime: it needs
to be wound up once

every seven days or so, equally
in two places: one place

takes care of the chimes and one
does the time-train

mechanism. Wouldn't it be fine
if we could be renovated

as effectively as a mantel clock?
Now, oh my how time

flies, the nine-o'clock hour — but
when our mechanism runs down

that's pretty much it, I guess, unless
somebody

working in a white coat
late under fluorescent lights

in a stem cell research lab
figures out how

to make a difference.

Threading the Needle

The wind is working
up the eaves; a twig on a branch
of the redbud tree out back scratches
siding outside above my head and

National Public Radio breaks the morning dark
with a fellow's mellow voice. Roll
with it, friend: if you're reading this
to find me out you won't

be disappointed and you might be
discouraged from reading more.
Like the old saw, how many threads
does it take to wrap a mummy? Well, one

of course, but the length depends
on the size of the mummy, the mean
diameter of the thread, the thickness
of the wrap in question, et cetera. Like I've said

before, learn to enjoy
variance. And learn to see
what's inside: reverse
the process, more or less

to unwind. In class today
for example I learned
students sometimes will rise
to a challenge but their main job as they see it

is to get me to give them points
and my job as I see it
is to get them to learn. Well,
this condition generates

dynamics: things you think
will move left don't
and the reciprocal's true, as well. Everything's
always in a rush: the end-of-semester rat-test

is breathing down our necks, it will happen
tomorrow and it will blur
with yesterday's lab. The rats
digitigrade in life are now

on their backs, gizzards
et al. up and mostly out
under fluorescent lights they look
so grim, squinty little pink eyes closed mostly

like the flu came through. But you can tell
now I'm wandering: the class
is closed, the grades
got plumped up as best I could and here

near the end of the semester
or the poem or the beginning
of today or somewhere
smack in my life I'm poised:

but
the left sock needs
pulling up a bit to match the right,
I can feel it.

Rat Dissection

For lab this week, the white rat—
Rattus norwiegicus: this was life,
respect it. Outside
on the female white rat find

twelve nipples, six by two. They grow
to produce milk to feed the young and shrink
when she's not pregnant. Later the vestibule—the space
between the teeth and cheek but note now

vibrissae on each side of the head above
the mouth on masticular pads; and pink eyes
plus eyelids, nictating membrane,
pinnae, the external part of the ear. A quick look

inside: see, teeth on the top and bottom,
four incisors for gnawing, twelve molars
for grinding. The uvula
hangs in the back of the throat like a little pink

punching bag: it goes up to block off
the nasal cavity during,
for example, vomiting. Don't confuse it
with vulva or the car. Opening

the jaws wide later you will cut back
from the angle of the jaw
with the blunt-tipped blade of the scissors
inside the mouth, through bone.

Find the epiglottis, covering the glottis, the opening
of the trachea, cartilaginous rings—

the larynx, structure
housing vocal cords. You'll work then

just anterior of the urogenital orifice. Cut
a small hole through the skin, the abdominal muscles,
carefully
past the diaphragm, letting

the abdominal cavity see light (some
preservative may leak out here). Find the liver—
it's the largest organ, wrapped
around the esophagus; count the lobes. Locate

the purplish spleen, the creamy pancreas
nestling the stomach. You will be responsible
tomorrow for knowing this
and much more. You will be graded

not just for knowing structure but for
neatness of dissection. The twenty-eight
students are rapt: they stare
at the dripping rat held up by the gloved hand.

Law of Chemistry

A shank of black hair hangs over his face
holding his anger in.
His glasses are pushed
low on his nose
letting his irritation out.
Frustration boils. Molecules want to
steam out at non-standard volume,
pressure, Mr. Damn

Avogadro can take his dumb gas laws
or not, who the hell cares?

    I try again. It is
all in dynamic balance, I say —
the temperature, the pressure,
the volume,

the CD is too much for me;
squeeze to increase pressure
and of course volume gets

turned down, add heat,
molecules jiggle faster and
anger happens and if
pressure is constant
the volume goes up. More heat,
       more volume or
           more pressure
the damn rap is too loud
      I react. First:

work it out
to standard temperature and pressure.
Cool, to correct

for differences, then go

from volume to moles,
from moles to molecules.
    Just
think like a molecule, I waggle my fingers.

His eyes smoke.
They are beautiful but he will not
let himself work past his anger.

A New Way to Generate Respect

Can't decide—
what to do: walk outside
early, thick fog, still dark;
birds
not yet singing
and the few sounds
of morning muffled. But still

hope: the day is poised
along a long summer axis of longing
and then
inside again, by accident I find it

in *Science News* online—I read
African dung beetles navigate by inspecting the angle
of polarized moonlight. How clever
given the less desirable aspects of their
hard-shell jobs—who'd want it,
dung, that is, fresh
or less. But here
investigators report the beetles took a squiggly path
when there was no moon but turned right or left
on cue if a polarizing filter was held
between them and the moon, allowing them to orient
the proper way. I must say there's more:

a USDA scientist said, for example,
these beetles could save
U.S. farmers up to two billion dollars a year by restoring
grazing land—recycling nitrogen
normally lost to the atmosphere
and by reducing the populations of flies
that stunt the growth of livestock.
And in Oklahoma, they say a rancher counted

eleven species of dung beetles on his land:
"Once the cattle have vacated the paddock," he reported,
"within 48 hours there is no manure left."
Wow, I think, maybe we could use these guys
to generate respect: maybe we could sic them
on political diatribe.

Bewept with Disrespect

The sonofabitch old dog has dug
in the flower garden again:
humping her shaggy back,
she takes the job
seriously, gives me
no respect, she just wants

the *Hosta*, the *Vinca minor*, the slick-leafed *Gardenia*
out by the roots,
or in the case of the delicate ferns
scattered now
out by their rhizoids, root-like
enough to qualify as roots, damn

she cannot be deterred
by wire, stones or potted plants deployed
as barricades to such abomination.
By manifesting her desire she creates
her cool garden bed, she destroys
even my capacity to think or write.

It Lives

1

Today the forest under the leaves
reeks of scurry and swell, fern heave,

wet and move. But everything inside
the domain of technology has gone

nano this and super that. They're twanking
the algorithms of life. Reported

today, by electronic news,
a waxy wheat. It needs

no milling—just pour
hot water on it and it turns

to a crunchy gruel. What next?
Pigs that fly?

2

I find myself
stretched uncertain—no question

generating focus; no rod
of rectitude; no congregation,

constellation, grouping or gathering;
no aggregation; no adhesion or binding, no

settling in or damping off. A lumpy time
with time on hold.

3

Deep in a glossary of literary terms—
kenning, the recurrent use of a descriptive phrase

in place of an ordinary name:
the whale road, for the sea.

A few pages farther, the Great
Chain of Being: a world view

grounded in ideas about the nature of God,
a premise

imbued with three consequences,
these being

plentitude, continuity and gradation. From which
emerged the doctrine of philosophical optimism,

to which, on some days, I might subscribe.
The Great Chain of Being, by the way, is not far

from Hyperbole and Understatement. Oh, I love
this literary crap! By seeing

words piled high
it becomes so much easier to appreciate

mud under the sticks holding the pile up.

4

Waffling, wavering: I discover
T.S. Eliot described the term "objective correlative,"

a set of objects, a situation, a chain of events
(not the Great Chain of Being) established

by an author for the purpose of revealing
(in my words) some particular

emotion, the intent being to invoke
in readers the same emotion. Correlations

I note often are mistaken as credible
sufficient links to causality: scientific crap

full of sound and fury and signifying
you know what.

5

Struggling for an orchestrated conclusion —
a tapering off, some hesitation, some thinning out:

then continuing. Under "P" I find palinode,
a poem or poetic passage

in which the poet renounces or retracts
an earlier poem or type of subject matter.

No, I think, I won't do that: bring down
an edifice, or rip up or tear

the wheels off the gilded hearse, or defoliate
the locust tree in flower, I've got

more respect than that.

6

Yet under semiotics I learn
three classes of signs — icon,

index and symbol, the latter listed too
as a sign proper, and these

collectively are not far
from the Seven Deadly Sins. See,

I can't bring this
damned thing to sonnet form! Read it —

it lives
to bite its tail.

Dark Water

It is difficult to decide
how this thing should be
fractured or cut: parts want to cleave
from the embryonic; groups of cells
established by mitotic divisions
want to break off—clusters
related to function, each one
imbued with a crystal will
or won't, each one

drags in uncertainty—parts
I don't know, pieces that won't
fit or which are fit
for mold only, snuggled to microscopic
hyphae glistening in wet soil

where they have a small chance, at least,
to live, feel grit and taste
molecules leaking from bacterial cells;
things move out
respecting the laws

of thermodynamics: steady
she goes, each thing
has a half-life; a period of time
during which it is
what it is, and after which,
on average, it is not—

it transforms: decays, undergoes
hydrolysis or photolysis, or randomly loses
an atom here or there, jiggled off

by accident, letting the thing
down to a more stable form. We know this
as certainly as we know gravity
attracts masses to one another in relation
to their individual masses and to the square
of the distance between the masses.

Yes, out she goes, day after day
to the well to fetch
what can be fetched
from a good well: dark water,
and the echo of a pebble dropped.

Makoto

Truth & Sincerity

Trickster Rules

It was near noon, and the warm air rising from the weedy field bordering the Blue River was buzzing with orthopterans—grasshoppers and their ilk. With each step we took, they burst up and away in various directions from the weeds. Some had gray-green bodies and coarse black accordion wings edged delicately in green; others were greener, sleeker, with more angular bodies; and others still were dusty-green, sturdy-bodied conventional hoppers sporting yellow underbellies and roguish yellow stripes on their oversized rear legs. Despite this diversity, their flights inevitably seemed clownish, in addition to forceful: a tremendous leaping take-off from some waist-high stem or leaf, arrow-straight initially, but terminating in a clumsy spoof of natural perfection. Some, for example, crash landed tumbling as they hit the earth; a few thumped literally head-first into tree trunks or bushes. Their objective clearly was quick escape, not nicety. Their chaotic bursting leaps might be viewed as elegant displays of apparent incompetence, I thought, or perhaps evolutionary manifestations of fuzzy success.

We piled our first load of sampling gear in shadows under the trees along the river bank, then trudged back through the buzzing field to the vehicles for more. On a previous visit to streams near the Kansas City Plant, in Kansas City, Missouri, we had been rained out.[1] Now, on this return visit, there seemed to be little chance of rain. The earth was dry and the leaves of the sycamore trees near the water's edge were at their late-summer coarsest, worn and starting to yellow. The leaves of the poison ivy, in shadow under the bank-side trees, were large and dusty; they had lost their youthful shine.

We were here with a crew of eight to finish sampling the fish, aquatic invertebrates and chemical water-quality conditions in Indian Creek and the Blue River, at the request of the environmental manager for the Department of Energy's Kansas City Plant. The issue leading to this request seemed straightforward: the Kansas City Plant is a production facility that releases a goodly amount of waste waters to each of the two streams, and was under stiff regulatory pressure by the state to reduce or eliminate concentrations of chlorine in these waste waters, so as to prevent possible damage to stream-dwelling organisms. Interestingly, the source of the chlorine in the waste waters was drinking water. In Kansas City, and in most other cities in the United States, water destined to be used for drinking is deliberately chlorinated at water treatment plants to kill bacteria—a treatment required by law, ensuring the water is safe for human consumption. But, ironically, concentrations of chlorine needed to kill bacteria in drinking water are also sufficient to kill fish, algae and aquatic invertebrates. And, like most toxic pollutants, it is far easier to add chlorine to water than it is to take it out.

We had been asked to provide data on ecological and chemical conditions in the two streams, upstream and downstream of the Kansas City Plant waste water release points, with the idea that the plant managers might use the data to apply for a waiver of their chlorine-release limit, delineated in their waste water discharge permit. If a chlorine-release waiver was not granted, the plant would be forced either to implement very costly in-plant plumbing changes, to the tune of hundreds of thousands of dollars, or to add chlorine-degrading chemicals to the waste waters near their point of release. However, if ecological impacts from the chlorine presently being released to the streams were negligible, the latter option would make no environmental sense, because the addition of chlorine-consuming chemicals to the waste waters would likely be more damaging, environmentally, than the chlorine that the chemicals were designed to remove. It was one of those uncomfortably topsy-turvy, damned-if-you-do, damned-if-you-don't situations that unfortunately is altogether too common in the search for truth. In the realm of environmental regulations, it is not unusual to find festering thickets of laws that run at odds with each other.

Fish living in streams can tell the truth about water-quality conditions without talking: they do not run at odds with each other; they do not fester like a thicket of laws. And this is why backpack shockers, chest waders and long-handled dip-nets were among the items we had lugged from the vehicles to the stream bank. Tools of the trade. A fiberglass bathtub-sized barge with strapped-on wheels (removed for use in water) contained a heavy-duty gasoline-powered generator capable of producing an electrical field strong enough to stun fish, even in waist-deep water. Backpack shockers with smaller gasoline-powered generators were used by persons in waders, working closer to the banks.

Fish stunned by electroshocking were scooped quickly from the stream with dip-nets and transferred first to buckets containing stream water, amended with an anesthetizing chemical, then later to in-stream "fish pens" made from seines, where they were allowed to recover. It was a noisy, jocular activity, reminiscent of an Easter egg hunt. Those wielding the dip-nets worked close to those wielding the shocker anodes, totally intent, plunging the nets down into the water to collect fish bodies flashing briefly from around rocks or snags or thrashing quickly near the water's surface, stung from a deep pool by the electric current. Channel catfish, brown bullhead, a golden shiner, long-ear sunfish, stoneroller minnows, bluegill sunfish, largemouth bass, and a few carp, some nearly as big as your arm, rolling to the water's surface, stiff and half-stunned from shocking, wonderfully orange-gold and heavy, gasping in the net.

We worked upstream slowly, through pools where the water depth sometimes approached the tops of our chest-high waders, and through ankle-deep riffles, probing the rocks and snags with long-handled, ring-shaped anodes. A few slender madtoms, a log perch, and finally, even a Johnny darter showed up. Twenty-one species, in all, from the eighty-meter reach of stream. A number not indicative of a pristine midwestern system, perhaps, where one might expect thirty or more species, but not too bad, either. Certainly it was a greater number than one might expect from a highly polluted, chlorine-blasted stream. And several of the species we caught were considered by fish ecologists to be pollution intolerant, providing a bit more evidence for generally favorable ecological conditions.

It always surprises me to see so many fish—buckets of fish!—from a turbid stream like this. From above, the muddy water moves in slow gyres, quietly, steadily, hardly winking under coins of sunlight speckling through the leafy canopy overhead. It offers little hint of the quick, darting activity below. I wonder, sometimes, what it must be like for fish living among the rocks and stones and woody snags in a turbid stream: cool and gloomy, and the pressure of the water—pushing, caressing, nudging with silent fingers, coiling around rocks and stones, carrying a bit of scent of things it had come into contact with farther upstream. I am reminded of the poem "The Bitter World of Spring," by William Carlos Williams:[2]

> . . . And casting an eye
> down into the water, there, announced
> by the silence of a white
> bush in flower, close
> under the bridge, the shad ascend,
>
> midway between the surface and the mud,
> and you can see their bodies
> red-finned in the dark
> water headed, unrelenting, upstream.

On shore, when collection was complete, the fish were hand scooped individually from the pens and weighed and measured; they were examined for physical conditions that might indicate poor water-quality conditions: body lesions, sores, tumors, the presence of external parasites or fin-rot. Then they were released, thrashing and wiggling, to the stream from which they came.

Standing in shallow water near the stream's edge, watching this activity, I thought about the possibility of their confusion—first, the tingling stun of electricity that sought them out from friendly crevices among the rocks, then the burst of light as they were netted and brought momentarily into the air, stunned; their senses fogging quickly due to the anesthetic in the bucket, and later, their abrupt transfer to a pen, for recovery before release. Confusion, disarray, chaos . . .

And suddenly, there it was again—just as I stood there, doing nothing but watching, the word chaos crept in. Elusive and slippery as a fish, it burst up like an orthopteran unexpectedly from the weeds, disrupting the innate human desire for order. But this time the Trickster was caught. We are here, I thought, netting fish we cannot see from turbid water, to make pronouncements about the quality of water here and upstream around the bend, a place we cannot discern; we busy ourselves sorting these fish out, by species and size, not knowing anything about their history; we are occupied in tabulating their numbers and weights, developing comfort, documenting pattern. This is our job today, I thought: to establish honesty through the pursuit of truth; to push back the sense of disorder, while a few clouds above drift carelessly on high, constantly changing the amounts and colors of the light filtering through the trees, the light sparkling on the water's surface, the water's surface slow-swirling, coiling this way and that as it moves downstream, intermittently steady under the force of gravity.

The "aha" emerging from personal insight into a problem is the word that jumps out to express the sense of satisfaction that results when the area of underlying perceived pattern suddenly becomes greater than the area under immediate investigation. Whatever else chaos is, it is pattern clouding. So it is chaos that is both the enemy and close friend of a scientist. And ever the Trickster,[3] whose teasing whim sometimes blows a bit of chaos away, letting our perception expand, or drags in an extra bit of chaos, reducing clarity. We should learn to work with the Trickster in college, I think. I can see it now—a punnish course title, "Trickster Rules: 101." In the classroom, a bespeckled professor, wild haired, of course, in ill-fitting slacks and a misbuttoned shirt, either mumbling or over-loud, in a monotonic drone or a thickly accented voice, lectures in a rising and falling cadence, pointing, with a log-linear model wooden pointer, to equations incomprehensibly scribbled on the blackboard, a state-of-the-art green laser pointer in his shirt pocket.

Then, while standing there watching the fish crew finish their work and whimsically musing, something thumped my chest just above the top of my waders. Startled, looking down, I saw, looking up, a sleek pure-green orthopteran, clinging perfectly to my shirt. It was almost motionless, katydid-like, nearly an inch and a half in length, with long antenna arching gracefully from the head, back, over the thorax: the left rear leg was being pulled slowly up and in, closer to the body, even as I watched. The muscles—I could almost see them, somehow in my mind's eye—the tiny muscles, attached to the interior surfaces of the exoskeletal leg, were contracting, enervated by smaller neurons, pale threads, the firing of which involved the active flux of sodium and potassium ions. And within each muscle cell, hundreds of mitochondria worked smoothly to produce the energetically rich organic compounds a muscle cell needs to do its work, just like in my body, with the concurrent influx of oxygen atoms and glucose molecules as raw materials, and the near-steady efflux of carbon dioxide and water, the waste. And I swear in that instant as I saw those things, just before the creature leaped, it looked up and grinned.

---

1. Stewart, A. J. 1999. Bridges, rivers, respect and power. Pp. 237–240. In: Ivie, D. and L. M. LaChance (eds.). *Breathing the Same Air: An East Tennessee Anthology*. Celtic Cat Publishing, Knoxville, TN. 318 pp.
2. Williams, W. C. 1985. "The Bitter World of Spring." In C. Tomlinson, ed. *William Carlos Williams: Selected Poems*. New Directions Books, New York, NY. 302 pp.
3. Combs, A. and M. Holland. 1996. *Synchronicity: Science, Myth, and the Trickster*. Marlowe & Company, New York, NY. 184 pp.

Fat as the Moon

When my kids were young
I'd torture them

routinely with lies. Example:
when the luminescent moon

was half-full and high as dusk
gallumped the ridge, like now

"Look," I said once, pointing. "See that jet
with the red and green winking lights, moving fast

from east to west? See? It's flying
higher than the moon." Brief

analysis, followed by something like
"Yeh, Dad, right." Sarcasm

the prevalent response. So
in slender retrospect: did this

unholy dumping of nonsense
do good? Well, who's to know? They're smart

but they might have become that
anyway. They're suspicious

of stated facts, as they should be—
but they might have become

that way by themselves, too.
Folding

my arms against the cold
now looking up at the half-fat moon I can't guess

or second-guess
what I did then—

the truth is behind me
but it's in me, too.

An Honest Mistake

Last week, a 68-year-old man hunting
for white-tailed deer took aim, let fly and killed
an elk with one shot—a big one, brought in
three months before and released

to help
start a herd in east Tennessee
hills and woods. The man
I heard later figured the problem out

fast and got busy quick
calling for help on his cell phone, and he took
two nitroglycerin pills
right there in the field, to keep

himself out of more trouble. I can imagine
he said oh, shit
this ain't no deer, dammit, no
or it's the biggest one I ever saw

with sticky blood oozing from the gaping hole
trickling down the warm side staining
the yellow leaves. It's not clear
what will happen next: the court case

is scheduled for next month; they'll show
glossies, I expect, of white-tailed deer
and elk side by side, and ask
do these two animals look the same

to you? That's different
as night and day from looking
down a rifle barrel's sight, letting
the breath out

delicately as an animal steps
from behind a bush, just
squeezing the trigger, letting
the sound roll out, knocking you back.

The Truth

1

Science staggers over the daisy meadow
like a sick cow: stupid-drooling and wild-staring,
she crushes a path (*statistical, final*) between fact and how.

2

The subtle angle of a bean's new head relates
somehow to the

    : explosiveness :

of the embryonic eight-celled bullet
coiled in the pistil.
There's a strange and shimmering wavelength
to the (shy-blue) skink,
a

    ** *curious* **

molecular shape to octopus ink.

3

My students,
come gather 'round the slick white porcelain tabletop; spread out
these sad entrails: they're . . .

    (poke, poke)

. . . from a predator, I think.

Here, for example: this wad of hair—
a wet and tailed grayish fur-ball

    (a mouse?

protein? calories? vitamins?)

      [: brief puzzlement :]

So, let's make it neutral, — a trophic link.

    But:

did it give life willingly,
singing a quiet prayer-song
of love and joyful satisfaction as —
(in that fractional last instant)
ivory teeth crushed sweetly through
intricate tiny vertebrae, neurons exploding
perfect in that final glorious
release from anti-entropy?

Or was the decision
fearful and more darkly made—
that is,
an unfortunate circumstance?

4

Here's truth:
ponds are slow to ice in winter
and, in spring, the morel pushes up through downed wet leaves
across a single moon-dark night.

Belly of the Beast

Well, in today's news, unhappy event, another man
beheaded. Or decapitated. I don't know
why the word is not deheaded, just
one of the quirky
aspects of the language, probably.

And not to make light of the situation, and yes,
to show sympathy for the family I'll stop
this topic here. But still
truth connects: what happens
there with a whisper-sharp blade
reverberates here, in the heart and the head and

jeez you see

them damned molecules are at it again:
    jiggling
information from one place
to another
instantly. If there's anything
to teleportation, these little things
can do it
with their eyes closed

tight. Come on,
come on, please, I ask,
how can I get this thing started? Whip
it up, crank the volume, turn
the gizzard on high. Somewhere today
I learned that tsunamis are almost

invisible in the open ocean: the wave
exposes its back and grows only when the belly feels
the bottom coming up or the water
getting shallow, but
right there, just behind the invisible
belly of the beast, at the air-water
interface, an interference is
set up. From space, a line of darker water

becomes visible, racing
on the water's surface, revealing
the tsunami's path. Another example
of an invisible thing

made visible with the right tool. Words
are like that — they convey
snippets of truth and love and

outside my window, right now, at six
twenty-three p.m. exactly
within the leatherleaf bush a tree frog calls.

He hesitates, listens,
calls again.

Bias

Sometimes I get too wrapped up
in looking at things: you know

the stereotypic introverted scientist,
the guy who can't step back to see

the bigger picture. A dangerous flaw
in the psyche, perhaps — something stuck

in the genes. But if you don't look
hard, hell, you'll see

only what filters in by pre-
programmed neuronal synapses

in the brain, and brains then don't work
worth a damn, so bias

oh, yes, has a picnic: ham
sandwiches, fried chicken,

potato salad, kosher dills,
the works.

Brier Creek

Months later I find an undated note to self
in my yellow *Rite-in-the-Rain* field notebook,
crabbed in pencil: "Just a way of cutting."
Cutting what? I try to remember

the gray conglomerate
of fossilized shells and rounded stones
pressed into the fine-grained shale
slabs on pool bottoms, the channel
incised deeply by the force of water
through time: fifty thousand years
perhaps, until now
this stream — Brier Creek —
slips through pools and sparkles
warm over riffles and here

on the bank again, I'm feeling
deeply sleepy but perfectly awake

overlooking a gravel bar pitched up
by last spring's flood and the sun
cracking now over the leaning banks
and the scabby-barked sycamores
practically holding their breaths it seems
possible at last to ask:
dear God, if there is
something I am supposed to do,

tell me so I can do it.

Einstein Was Right Again

Perusing reports this morning I was surprised to see
THERMONUCLEAR FLICKER

a headline I mistakenly read first as
THERMONUCLEAR FUCKER.

Just for a moment, of course — the L and the I
are, like, you know, so close

to touching and this
error in visual translation set off

all kinds of wild ideas I won't
go into here. Let it suffice to say

I said it, although I would not
say it at work, oh no, it's a good thing

I'm on my own turf now. But
back to the other facts: Einstein

big guy, was right again. The greatest
spin-rate of pulsars

is less than the theoretical limit
of 760 revolutions per second — what a flicker

rate — how they go
that fast I can't imagine but Einstein

smart guy, saw somehow
it must be true.

Lost Water

With prodding I try
sincerely to write tighter: I eliminate

articles, prepositions,
adjectives, almost everything

except verbs; insert
new words like tersity

to twist tongues,
pepper the page but

they trickle through
my fingers

like water lost
from a cupped hand.

Finale on the Finger

Today I took the hurt finger
to a doctor, blowing
two hours but I tried at least
to have fun. He was running
late as doctors do, so I said

Doctor, I can get you
back on schedule single-handedly,
with one finger. Ha!

He just studied
the left hand held up and bent
the finger firmly to the left, away
from the body, away
from the thumb, truth is, oh jeez I jumped

right up from the chair, woojums
it hurt so much again. He said
Oh, it's not broken, just sprained and these things
can take months to heal. So much
I thought for fun. That night

Brussels sprouts: I cut off
their stems while holding
the little bodies
one after another, cupping them
in the left hand as best I could; I cut

an X deeply into each
little cabbage-head brain
from the ventral side, doctoring them

lightly with salt and butter,
dusting them with pepper. How's that,
I asked each one as I finished it, waiting

briefly for an answer. Tell me,
did that hurt?

You Know You Never Know

Flakes whirling fast at first then slow
after the sun went down and the clouds
    squatted: yes,
that is a word I know I should drag
into the present tense, the clouds
    are doing it
still: and yes, that's how the flakes are falling
right now, still. One can always ask

where does the wind go when it goes
or has gone? Ah, so many questions get waylaid
as we age: good ones get set up
and knocked down, answers racked up
as prizes. We think

we know a thing and if we do, well
that's fine. It's like the tangled sketch I made

yesterday, for a young girl down the road:
grade school science homework—her family tree.
Her mom it turned out had three children, each
fathered by a different man. It made me think
at first the mom might be, well,

you know, unsteady. But then I thought
hey, maybe she's steady
in some way, like what she makes
for breakfast—oatmeal
six times a week, or maybe in some
minor characteristic
of how she drives. You know,

past or present, what's truth,
you never know.

News by Phone

Last night my sister called
tinny voice from far away
to let me know
on Monday, Dad
took a header: that is

on his morning wobbling walk
crossing the street a pothole bit him: he went
down on the road, gashing the head, hurting
a shoulder. There he was, clawing
up to sitting, a person running to help

get him to the curb. At last
the ambulance with its bitter lights.
Confused but adamant he refused
to get in — once he got
into an ambulance, you know,
he knew
he would be dead. Lord,

there's nothing
quite like a hypochondriac. Finally

in the hospital they got him
settled down, stitched up, shot
a dozen X-rays of the neck and head
and chest and asked him

      (oh, what a mistake!)

did he have cancer, maybe,
there's a small spot on the left lung.

When Electricity Goes Off at Night

At first
a feeling of loss: insecurity,
wariness. A need

to keep the eyes wide open. At a small level
in this sudden silence I'm almost aware:
a molecule diffuses across a gap, bumps

another molecule,
starts
a tiny cascade. In a rush

small enough to be of no significant consequence
the cascade slows, concludes,
the gradient builds back: drifting

with gradients, or against; being worked on
by carrier molecules, anti-diffusion
devices expending ATP energy

or zigzagging uphill
energetically speaking,
restoring potential, gradually

eyes now almost seeing
in the dark.

Recalibration Might be Needed

No crystal
in the air outdoors, she's a humid old goat
today breathing
wet air into the face, stinking

sweet of hay, summer berries and so many
diversified leaves—narrow or wide or highly dissected;
margins lobed, entire or toothed, moving
on to old coffee, not thick
as blood, impenetrably dark and the word

inscrutable rises while I keep scrabbling
into one of the many wheels
of things: the nave or a spoke,
banging the head or a leg
on the way down, skinning a knuckle—
though along the way I pick up

a few tricks; tessellate them
to old tricks; consider the turns it takes
to get from one place to another, question
self to the point
of unadulterated reconciliation, love that word, the
six-syllable length and bouncy back, could be
a snake in the make

ing. Oh my,
how low one can stoop, I think,
referring to me. I really should
get back to Wright's *Above the River*: catch
the flavor, get the drift—some

recalibration might be needed: a new calf,
for example; a white horse, the beautiful
Ohio River, his work
like a room-temperature
cantaloupe cut: orange
surprise, exposed
suddenly, wet inside and the skin
wrinkled, white seeds cling
to the thready firmament,
truth, maybe, the last hope.

Perspective on the Destruction of Mossy Grove

From a helicopter later they gave facts: showed
where it had passed and said
it cut a swath a half-mile wide and six
miles long: they said
it sounded
louder than a train: they said a baby wrapped

in a blanket was sucked out
of the truck in which she was being carried
towards presumed safety by her grandfather, away

from the mobile home
terrified of the thing that roared at night
and the mobile home later was found unscathed
while the baby ended up
dead, across the field, face down
in water. And the grandfather, too, was killed
in his twisted truck. And they said

an eleven-year-old boy
showering in his house that night got picked up
and dropped
three hundred yards away in a church parking lot, scratched
and dizzy no doubt but otherwise
unharmed. He got busy
quick I guess looking for fig leaves. And Mossy Grove

they say thus
was in a night destroyed. The houses there
before became

shredded lumber, shingles, and concrete blocks
spread out and mixed up. They said

they couldn't have done it
like that with a bulldozer
huffing hard for a week. It was that
sudden. But from our house,

thirty miles southwest, we saw huge clouds that night
boiling dark, made luminous by lightning,

silent, moving east.

Two Sides of the Coin

Nine hundred-forty miles
east of Jakarta, Flores:

island of little people who lived
in caves like hobbits

as late as the 1500s, when Dutch sailors
arrived, saw them and took back

information I bet that spread
by diffusion in pubs to stories

in Ireland of leprechauns
hoarding gold. The garnet clarity

of things we think we know now
by close inspection of the physical

strips life from the delicate bones
of history: old wives' tales,

superstitions, mythology, magic, luck,
fables, rumors — our incandescent

fundamentals.

About the Author

Arthur Stewart is an ecologist, senior scientist, essayist and poet. He graduated from Northern Arizona University, then spent two years as a Peace Corps volunteer in Ghana. Upon returning to the U.S., he earned his Ph.D. at Michigan State University, then completed a postdoctoral fellowship at Oak Ridge National Laboratory in Oak Ridge, Tennessee. He taught aquatic ecology and conducted stream ecology research as an assistant professor at the University of Oklahoma, then returned to Oak Ridge National Laboratory to work as an aquatic ecologist and ecotoxicologist. He has authored or co-authored more than sixty articles and book chapters and has served as editor or associate editor for *Environmental Toxicology and Chemistry*, *Journal of the North American Benthological Society*, and *Ecotoxicology*. He is currently adjunct research professor at the University of Tennessee and lives in Lenoir City. Stewart's first collection of poems, *Rough Ascension and Other Poems of Science*, was published in 2003.

About the Book

This book was typeset in Adobe Garamond with Brioso display.
It was printed and bound by Thomson-Shore, Inc., Ann Arbor, Michigan, on 60# Thor Recycled White.

The calligraphic characters for Rei and Makoto were graciously provided by Eri Takase, master calligrapher of Takase Studios (www.takase.com).

Edited by Linda P. Marion
Design by Dariel Mayer
Cover art by Justin A. Dickerman-Stewart